The ARKANSAS LIBRARY BOOK:

📖 **A surprising guide to the unusual special collections in libraries across our state. For students, teachers, writers & publishers. INCLUDES EXTENSIVE INDEX + ACTIVITIES FOR STUDENTS**

by
Carole Marsh

Other Carole Marsh Books for Students, Writers & Publishers

THE ARKANSAS BOOKSTORE BOOK:
A surprising guide to our state's bookstores and their specialties for students, teachers, writers & publishers

THE ARKANSAS MEDIA BOOK: A useful guide to the newspapers, magazines, tv, radio and online computer media right out your back door

TOUCH TYPING IN TEN MINUTES!:
On Any Keyboard At Any Age

How To Produce (1-1000!) Books On Your Computer & Bind Them Professionally -- One At a Time!

How To Get Paid UP FRONT For Book Orders -- Even From the Big Guys!

THE WRITER'S PLAN: Reproducible Forms to Organize Your Writing for Pleasure and Profit

EVERREADY EDITORIAL: How To Write a Bestselling Book -- Each & Every Day!

PUBLISHING ON COMMAND: The Secrets of Gallopade Publishing Group's "Book Bakery" -- Which Produces 1,600 Books On-Demand Each & Every Day!

Self-Publishing By the Seat of Your Pants:
If Not You, Who?, If Not Now, When?, If Not, Why Not?!

THE BIG INSTRUCTION BOOK OF SMALL BUSINESS: Arkansas Edition

The Little-Known, Never-Told Secrets of
BOOK DISTRIBUTION: For Authors & Small Presses

Table of Contents

✎ A Word From the Author 4

👓 How To Use a Special Library 5

☞ How To Use this Book 6

📕 ARKANSAS LIBRARIES
& THEIR SPECIAL COLLECTIONS 8

📓 Special Activities for Teachers to Use With Students 23

〰 Glossary 24

🎓 Bibliography 25

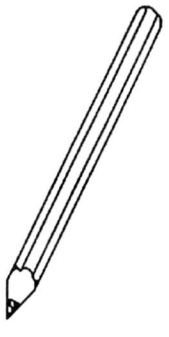

🚗 SPECIAL LIBRARY RESOURCE FORM 26

A Word From the Author

My fondest memory, from the time I was very, very young, was the library. It was a special place my mommy took me. There were hundreds of books, and best of all, the nice people actually let me take them home! My favorite library was a bright, sunny one with lots of plants and big chairs. The books I remember with excitement from this library are *Tales Told Under the Blue Umbrella*, *The Secret Garden*, *National Geographic*, and *On the Beach*. I read them all before I was seven years old.

Even today, I associate specific libraries with a favorite book: an old typeface book (one set of letters was made out of twigs!) from a tiny, private library in Tryon, North Carolina . . . *Outlaws of the Sea* and other pirate books from the one-room Bath library. I still remember with awe my first visit to the family genealogy library in Salt Lake City (I planned to stay 10 minutes and left 10 hours later!) It's not a bit surprising that I turned out to be a writer and a publisher.

So convinced am I that library experience is critical to the educational success of children, that I wrote a book, *Poetry to Read to the Unborn Baby*. Many libraries use this book in a reading program with expectant parents and issue the child-to-be's first library card at that time. We're even starting our own Gallopade company library. Its special collection will be my 1,600+ books (so far!) which include over 30 special titles for each American state + Washington, DC.

The ticket to all the information, knowledge, skill, laughter, excitement, and enlightenment and discovery that we can devour -- the library card -- is priceless. A library -- and the desire, know-how and permission to use it -- is for a lifetime and one of our most precious resources. A love of libraries and the materials they contain is a universal emotion, understood in every language and by any culture.

To me, *every* library is special. But I hope this book makes it easy for you to discover and use the many surprising special collections that are just out the back door! How enhanced travel is when a stop by the local library is part of your itinerary.

Like many others, I'm distressed at the state of and status of our libraries today. As a citizen, do what you can to ensure that the library that we have known, loved and benefitted so immensely by will exist in no less a state of respect and readiness for generations to come.

Happy reading and researching! See you in the stacks,

Carole Marsh

👓 How To Use a Special Library

First, know exactly what you need from this library. Do you just want to browse -- look around and see what they have? Or do you want to use their reference books? Do you need to check out one book or many? What specific subject are you interested in? What specific author(s)? Try to be as prepared as possible when you visit a special library. Why? Because then, the librarian can help you much faster and easier. This will save you both time and frustration.

Next, contact the library by mail or phone first. Find out if the library is open to the public. If not, but you know exactly what type of information you're looking for -- and you have a good reason (you're a writer, reporter, researcher, doing a special project, work in that field, an alumni of that school, only in town for a single day, etc.) -- you may find you can get special permission to use the library, even if it's "private". Be sure and talk to the person who can give you this authority before you give up. If you aren't able to get access to the library, they may be able to suggest an alternate way you can borrow materials, such as through interlibrary loan. You'll also want to find out the current days and hours the library is open.

When you visit a special library, make the most of your time. Be prepared before you go. Ask the librarian to point out the main areas of the library or direct you to the specific subject you're interested in. The library may have a brochure describing its layout and services; get this ahead of time if you can. Use the reference books that can't be checked out first, then borrow the books that can be loaned. Many libraries offer a temporary library card for a small fee. I have checked out books this way when traveling and later returned the books (on time and in good condition!) by mail.

Thank the librarians for their assistance. Compliment them on what you liked and make suggestions for additional materials they might carry, if any. Make a donation?--

⌒⌒How To Use This Book

This book was developed for our in-house editorial use at Gallopade Publishing. It proved to be too fascinating and useful not to share! Here are a few special notes about the logic behind the simple way this book is set up and how to use it:

Using the SPECIAL LIBRARY RESEARCH FORM at the end of this book (you're welcome to make additional copies), scan through the library listings. Make notations in the appropriate columns of the subjects you're interested in + the library location + the page number.

What you're doing is creating *your own* specialized index to the libraries and special collections in our state that you are interested in. You can create one list, one for each subject, or even a list for a particular city or town.

What do you do once you have your form completed? I keep mine in a notebook in my car. Then, when I plan a trip, or am on the road, I refer to this form for a quick and easy reference. Students can use their form as a tool for researching a term paper. I'm sure you'll find uses just as special as your interests. Go ahead, get carried away!

One reason I want you to read or scan through the listings is so you can discover the many specialty libraries you never heard of before, as well as special subjects you never knew you were interested in *until* you saw a great source of information!

You'll also wonder why every library in the state is not listed -- especially some of the larger, well-known ones. The reason is that we were unable to get any specifics about *special* collections in those libraries. This book is not to steer you toward general fiction and non-fiction, but we will be adding every library and special collection brought to our attention, as well as new libraries we might not have discovered during our special collection "safari".

Let this book be just the beginning of your special library collections listing. If this is your own personal copy of this book, add additional libraries or special collections on the blank facing pages.

WHY DIDN'T WE LIST THE LIBRARY STREET ADDRESS OR PHONE NUMBER? BECAUSE AS A COMPANY WHO MAILS TO EVERY LIBRARY IN THE UNITED STATES EACH YEAR, WE HAVE DISCOVERED THAT THEY MOVE AROUND, CHANGE POST OFFICE BOXES AND PHONE NUMBERS. THE SAFEST AND FASTEST WAY TO MAKE MAIL OR PHONE CONTACT WITH A PARTICULAR LIBRARY IS TO CALL INFORMATION FOR THEIR NUMBER & PHONE THEM DIRECTLY. THEY CAN THEN TELL YOU ABOUT THEIR CURRENT STATUS. THIS CAN INCLUDE WHETHER THEY'RE UNDER RENOVATION (AND THE SPECIAL COLLECTIONS ARE IN STORAGE) . . . THE SPECIFIC DAYS AND HOURS THEY ARE OPEN (MANY CUTBACKS THESE DAYS) . . . AND IF THEY HAVE ANY INFORMATION THEY CAN SEND YOU SUCH AS THEIR LIBRARY NEWSLETTER, HANDBOOK OR PUT YOU ON THEIR MAILING LIST TO RECEIVE NOTIFICATION OF ADDITIONS TO THEIR SPECIAL COLLECTIONS. WE'VE RUN INTO *EVERYTHING* AND PROMISE THAT THIS IS THE BEST WAY TO MAKE INITIAL CONTACT WITH A LIBRARY. THEN, GO! -- NOT ONLY WILL YOU PROBABLY DISCOVER JUST WHAT YOU WERE LOOKING FOR . . . BUT YOU'LL ALMOST CERTAINLY DISCOVER EXCITING TREASURES YOU NEVER EXPECTED! BE A SPORT -- TAKE A KID WITH YOU!

Gopher It!
ARKANSAS LIBRARIES WITH SPECIAL COLLECTIONS & AREAS OF INTEREST:

📖 CLARK COUNTY LIBRARY, Arkadelphia:
genealogy, DAR, Arkansas

📖 HENDERSON STATE UNIVERSITY LIBRARY, Arkadelphia:
rural education

📖 OUACHITA BAPTIST UNIVERSITY LIBRARY, Arkadelphia:
education, humanities, music, oral history, Sen. John McClellan papers, Arkansas Baptist State Convention

📖 ARKANSAS COLLEGE RESOURCE CENTER, Batesville:
Arkansas

📖 WHITE RIVER REGIONAL LIBRARY, Batesville:
Arkansas history

📖 ARKANSAS STATE UNIVERSITY, BEEBE LIBRARY, Beebe:

general collection

📖 BENTON SERVICES CENTER MEDICAL LIBRARY:
medical

📖 SALINE COUNTY PUBLIC LIBRARY, Benton:
Arkansas, art, architecture, history

📖 BENTONVILLE PUBLIC LIBRARY:
Arkansas, Benton County Democrat, large print, Northwest Arkansas genealogy

📖 MISSISSIPPI COUNTY LIBRARY SYSTEM, Blytheville:
general collection

📖 UNITED STATES AIR FORCE LIBRARY, Blytheville Air Force Base:
military

📖 SOUTHERN ARKANSAS UNIVERSITY TECH-LIBRARY, Camden:
general

📖 UNIVERSITY OF THE OZARKS LIBRARY, Clarksville:
Arkansas

📖 CENTRAL BAPTIST COLLEGE LIBRARY, Conway:
general

📖 **FAULKNER-VAN BUREN REGIONAL LIBRARY**, Conway:
Arkansas

📖 **HENDRIX COLLEGE LIBRARY**, Conway:
Arkansas Methodism, Arkansas

📖 **UNIVERSITY OF CENTRAL ARKANSAS LIBRARY**, Conway:
children's literature, Arkansas

📖 **PAUL SULLINS PUBLIC LIBRARY**, Crossett:
Arkansas history

📖 **ARKANSAS RIVER VALLEY REGIONAL LIBRARY**, Dardanelle:
general collection

📖 **DEWITT PUBLIC LIBRARY:**
general

📖 **SOUTH ARKANSAS ARTS CENTER LIBRARY**, El Dorado:
general

📖 **SOUTHERN ARKANSAS UNIVERSITY AT EL DORADO LIBRARY:**
general

📖 **UNION COUNTY LIBRARIES**, El Dorado:
Arkansas, genealogy, monographs, large print books, El Dorado

📚 **UNIVERSITY OF ARKANSAS FOR MEDICAL SCIENCES LIBRARY, El Dorado:**
medical sciences

📚 **ANTAEUS LINEAL RESEARCH ASSOCIATES LIBRARY, Fayetteville:**
anthropology, archaeology, medicine, war

📚 **OZARKS REGIONAL LIBRARY, Fayetteville:**
genealogy, blindness and physically handicapped, professional collection for dealing with handicaps, music albums, nursing home activity directors and schools with handicapped children

📚 **UNIVERSITY OF ARKANSAS FOR MEDICAL SCIENCES LIBRARY, Fayetteville:**
clinical medicine, clinical nursing

📚 **UNIVERSITY OF ARKANSAS LIBRARIES, Fayetteville:**
Arkansas, Arkansas authors, folklore, rare books, regional history, J. William Fulbright, Sen. Joe T. Robinson, chemistry, fine arts, physics

📚 **VETERANS ADMINISTRATION MEDICAL LIBRARY, Fayetteville:**
medicine, consumer health, nursing

📚 **DALLAS COUNTY LIBRARY, Fordyce:**
general

📖 EAST ARKANSAS COMMUNITY COLLEGE RESOURCE CENTER, Forrest City:
general

📖 FORREST CITY PUBLIC LIBRARY:
Arkansas

📖 FORT SMITH PUBLIC LIBRARY:
Fort Smith, Arkansas history and genealogy, blindness and physically handicapped

📖 SAINT EDWARD MERCY HOSPITAL LIBRARY, Fort Smith:
medical

📖 SEBASTIAN COUNTY LAW LIBRARY, Forth Smith:
law

📖 SPARKS HOSPITAL - UNIVERSITY OF ARKANSAS MEDICAL SCIENCES LIBRARY, Fort Smith:
medical

📖 WESTARK COMMUNITY COLLEGE LIBRARY, Fort Smith:
historical

📖 SCOTT-SEBASTIAN REGIONAL LIBRARY, Greenwood:
Arkansas, large print, gifted children

📚 **ASHLEY COUNTY LIBRARY**, Hamburg:
genealogy

📚 **POINSETT COUNTY LIBRARY**, Harrisburg:
general

📚 **NORTH ARKANSAS REGIONAL LIBRARY**, Harrison:
Arkansas history and genealogy, Boone County historical photographs

📚 **PRAIRIE COUNTY LIBRARY**, Hazen:
general

📚 **PHILLIPS COUNTY COMMUNITY COLLEGE LIBRARY**, Helena:
art, automotives, Delta Blues

📚 **PHILLIPS-LEE-MONROE REGIONAL LIBRARY**, Helena:
Arkansas, Helena and genealogy

📚 **SOUTHWEST ARKANSAS REGIONAL LIBRARY**, Hope:
general

📚 **GARLAND COUNTY COMMUNITY COLLEGE RESOURCE CENTER**, Hot Springs:
general

📚 **HOT SPRINGS FORESTRY RESEARCH CENTER LIBRARY**:
forestry

📖 TRI-LAKES REGIONAL LIBRARY, Hot Springs:
genealogy, Colonial doll house ('76 Heritage House), model, Bath House Row, oral history

📖 NATIONAL CENTER FOR TOXICOLOGICAL RESEARCH LIBRARY, Jefferson:
biochemistry, carcinogenesis, immunology, mutagenesis, teratology, toxicology

📖 ARKANSAS STATE UNIVERSITY LIBRARY, Jonesboro:
aeronautics, library science, children, legal resource, Midsouth Center for oral history

📖 CRAIGHEAD COUNTY & JONESBORO PUBLIC LIBRARY, Jonesboro:
genealogy, Arkansas

📖 CROWLEY RIDGE REGIONAL LIBRARY, Jonesboro:
blindness and physically handicapped

📖 UNIVERSITY OF ARKANSAS AREA HEALTH CENTER LIBRARY, Jonesboro:
medicine, medical sciences, nursing, pharmacology

📖 CHICOT COUNTY PUBLIC LIBRARY, Lake Village:
genealogy, minority studies

📖 ARKANSAS ARTS CENTER LIBRARY, Little Rock:

early American Jazz, political cartoons

📖 ARKANSAS BAPTIST COLLEGE LIBRARY, Little Rock:
general

📖 ARKANSAS DIVISION OF REHABILITATION SERVICES LIBRARY, Little Rock:
rehabilitation

📖 ARKANSAS GAZETTE NEWS LIBRARY, Little Rock:
Gazette from 1819 to present

📖 ARKANSAS GEOLOGICAL COMMISSION LIBRARY, Little Rock:
geology

📖 ARKANSAS POWER & LIGHT COMPANY LIBRARY, Little Rock:
utilities, deafness

📖 ARKANSAS SCHOOL FOR THE BLIND LIBRARY, Little Rock:
Arkansas, professional collection of materials on visual impairment and blindness, Kurzweil reading machine

📖 ARKANSAS SCHOOL FOR THE DEAF LIBRARY, Little Rock:
deafness

📖 ARKANSAS STATE HOSPITAL LIBRARY, Little

Rock:
nursing, psychiatry, psychology, rehabilitation, social work

📖 ARKANSAS STATE LIBRARY, Little Rock:
Arkansas, library services for the blind and physically handicapped, the South, Civil War, folklore, Ozarks, African-American history

📖 ARKANSAS STATE LIBRARY SERVICES FOR THE BLIND AND PHYSICALLY HANDICAPPED LIBRARY, Little Rock:
blindness, physically handicapped

📖 ARKANSAS SUPREME COURT LIBRARY, Little Rock:
law

📖 BAPTIST MEDICAL SYSTEM LIBRARY, Little Rock:
nursing, medicine, management resources, fiction, paramedic, physical and occupational therapy

📖 CENTRAL ARKANSAS LIBRARY SYSTEM, Little Rock:
genealogy, Little Rock history, sheet music, deafness, Charlie May Simon awards

📖 JOHN L. MCCLELLAN MEMORIAL VETERANS HOSPITAL LIBRARY, Little Rock:
health sciences

📚 METROPLAN (Metropolitan Area Planning Commission), Little Rock:
census records, city planning, transportation studies, water quality

📚 NATIONAL EDUCATION CORPORATION, ARKANSAS COLLEGE TECHNOLOGY LIBRARY, Little Rock:
electronics, computer programming

📚 PHILANDER SMITH COLLEGE LIBRARY, Little Rock:
Arkansas, African-American culture

📚 SAINT VINCENT INFIRMARY MEDICAL CENTER LIBRARY, Little Rock:
medicine

📚 UNITED STATES COURT OF APPEALS LIBRARY, Little Rock:
federal law

📚 UNIVERSITY OF ARKANSAS AT FAYETTEVILLE LIBRARY, Little Rock:
science technology, electronics, instrumentation

📚 UNIVERSITY OF ARKANSAS AT LITTLE ROCK LIBRARY:
Arkansas, Chet Locke, Winthrop Rockefeller, Charlie May Simon, US and European economic community

📚 UNIVERSITY OF ARKANSAS FOR MEDICAL SCIENCES LIBRARY, Little Rock:

pathology, history of medicine in Arkansas

📖 UNITED STATES AIR FORCE LIBRARY, Little Rock Air Force Base:
aeronautics, business and management, military

📖 LONOKE COUNTY LIBRARY, Lonoke:
general

📖 COLUMBIA-LAFAYETTE-OUACHITA-CALHOUN REGIONAL LIBRARY, Magnolia:
blindness, handicapped, large print books

📖 SOUTHERN ARKANSAS UNIVERSITY LIBRARY, Magnolia:
Arkansas

📖 HOT SPRING COUNTY LIBRARY, Malvern:
Arkansas, genealogy

📖 CRITTENDEN COUNTY LIBRARY, Marion:
general

📖 WHITE RIVER REGIONAL LIBRARY, Melbourne:
general

📖 SOUTHEAST ARKANSAS REGIONAL LIBRARY, Monticello:
Arkansas

📖 UNIVERSITY OF ARKANSAS-MONTICELLO

LIBRARY:
Arkansas, forestry

📚 CONWAY COUNTY LIBRARY, Morrilton:
general

📚 INTERNATIONAL LIBRARY, Morrilton:
agriculture, livestock, systems, public policy

📚 OZARK FOLK LIBRARY, Mountain View:
Ozark folklore, music & crafts, oral history

📚 MONTGOMERY COUNTY LIBRARY, Mount Ida:
general

📚 JACKSON COUNTY LIBRARY, NEWPORT:
Arkansas

📚 FIRST ASSEMBLY OF GOD LIBRARY, North Little Rock:
religion

📚 WILLIAM F. LAMAN PUBLIC LIBRARY, North Little Rock:
Arkansas, genealogy, railroading

📚 SHORTER COLLEGE LIBRARY, North Little Rock:
ethnic studies

📚 COMMUNITY METHODIST HOSPITAL LIBRARY, Paragould:
medicine, nursing

📖 **CROWLEY'S RIDGE COLLEGE LIBRARY,** Paragould:
religion

📖 **NORTHEAST ARKANSAS REGIONAL LIBRARY,** Paragould:
general

📖 **ARKANSAS DEPARTMENT OF CORRECTION LIBRARY,** Pine Bluff:
prison related

📖 **PINE BLUFF & JEFFERSON COUNTY LIBRARY SYSTEM,** Pine Bluff:
wildlife conservation, Arkansas and Mississippi Valley, genealogy with emphasis on Arkansas, North Carolina, South Carolina, Tennessee and Virginia

📖 **UNIVERSITY OF ARKANSAS, PINE BLUFF LIBRARY:**
agriculture, education, industrial arts, nursing, African-American, rare books, Arkansas

📖 **CLEVELAND COUNTY LIBRARY,** Rison:
general

📖 **ARKANSAS TECH UNIVERSITY LIBRARY,** Russellville:
Parks and recreation administration

📖 **HARDING UNIVERSITY LIBRARY,** Searcy:
oral history

📖 WHITE COUNTY PUBLIC LIBRARY SYSTEM, Searcy:
Arkansas history and literature

📖 GRANT COUNTY LIBRARY, Sheridan:
general

📖 JOHN BROWN UNIVERSITY RESOURCE CENTER, Siloam Springs:
general

📖 SILOAM SPRINGS PUBLIC LIBRARY:
general

📖 FISH FARMING EXPERIMENTAL LABORATORY, STUTTGART:
warm water fish culture, nutrition and diseases

📖 STUTTGART PUBLIC LIBRARY:
American Indians, antiques, Arkansas, genealogy

📖 TEXARKANA PUBLIC LIBRARY:
Arkansas and Texas

📖 UNIVERSITY OF ARKANSAS FOR MEDICAL SCIENCES LIBRARY, Texarkana:
medical sciences

📖 LAWRENCE COUNTY LIBRARY, Walnut Ridge:
general

📖 SOUTHERN BAPTIST COLLEGE LIBRARY, Walnut Ridge:

Arkansas, Southern Baptist Convention

📕 SOUTHWEST ARKANSAS REGIONAL ARCHIVES, Washington:
history of southwest Arkansas, Civil War

📕 WEST MEMPHIS PUBLIC LIBRARY:
general

📕 EAST CENTRAL ARKANSAS REGIONAL LIBRARY, Wynne:
general

Special Activities for Teachers to Use With

Students

✎Pretend there are no book classification systems, such as the Dewey Decimal. Have your students create an original system.

✎Have students do a biography of Andrew Carnegie. Let them focus on why he made libraries his special interest, his "rules" for contributing to a town's library, whether or not a Carnegie donation helped build any of the libraries in their town or state, and what difference this made to that community.

✎Let students do a biography of Melvil Dewey. What interesting and innovative ideas did he have? What was his book system based upon?

✎Have students compare the Dewey Decimal System and Library of Congress system. Have them research what an ISBN number is. Introduce them to *Books In Print* and *The American Library Directory*.

✎Have students pretend there are NO libraries -- not in the class, at school, in the community or anywhere. Assign the following project: a one-page paper on "The History of Civilization", to include at least 12 specific facts. No libraries, no books allowed. Now, go to it! Discuss the importance of libraries in history, to students today and tomorrow, and the sad status of many libraries today. (A reverse project would be to assign a simpler one-page subject, but all the facts must come from books. Then have them read their papers aloud. Stop them at each fact and ask, "Did you get this from a book?" If the answer is, "Yes", make them strike through it. Have them rewrite their papers with only the information left. Use the same discussion questions.)

✎Visit your local "special library collections"!

Glossary

Biographies: Books about people's lives.

Bookmobile: A "library on wheels" which takes books to people who cannot get to the library building, or where there may be no library.

Call Number: The combination of letters and/or numbers that identify a library book. You will find this number on the card catalog and then go to the stacks and look for the book with this same call number.

Catalog: The cards (or information on a computer) that describes the books in a library and their location.

Circulation desk, Check Out Disk, Charge Desk: Where you go with your books and library card to officially "borrow" them.

Fiction: Books created from the author's imagination.

Holdings: All the books, etc. a library has in its collection.

Incunabula: Books printed before the year 1501.

Interlibrary loan Most libraries can borrow a book you want from another library around their system, the state, or the country.

Microfilm, microfiche Information recorded on a special tape which is read through a special viewing machine.

Non-Fiction: Books based on true facts.

Periodicals: Magazines, for example.

Rare Books: Either very old books or books of which there are very few copies left.

Realia: Today at a library, you can not only borrow books, tapes or videos, but "real objects" as well, such as bird nests, live rabbits, paintings, sculpture, and many other things.

Reference: Books which can be used in the library, but not borrowed.

Stacks: The shelves where the books are stored.

Vertical File: A collection of pamphlets, pictures, articles and documents temporarily in a library collection.

Bibliography

FOR ADDITIONAL INFORMATION ON SPECIAL LIBRARIES & SPECIAL COLLECTIONS, CHECK THE FOLLOWING SOURCES:

The American Library Directory
Most libraries have a copy in their reference section. It has libraries of all types listed by state and town; Canadian libraries are also listed. It is published annually.

The Directory of Special Libraries & Information Centers
Published annually. This reference book includes major special libraries, research libraries, documentation centers, archives and more for the U. S. and Canada + a subject listing.

The Special Libraries Association (SLA)
Annually publishes a publications directory listing directories of special libraries published by SLA chapters or divisions, as well as other books about specific types of special libraries (such as map libraries) or libraries located in specific places (in research centers, for example). SLA is divided into various divisions such as aerospace, geography and map, etc. and offers different levels of membership, primarily for the student, professional, or retired special librarian. They can be reached at 1700 Eighteenth St, NW, Washington;, DC 20009, 202-234-4700.

Gallopade Publishing Group
Publishes a book like this one for each state + Washington, DC. Future editions include each Canadian province and various countries around the world. Gallopade also publishes a series of books about libraries in general, with editions for each state & Washington, DC. These books are especially useful with readers grades 4-12 since they give the history, geography, trivia and more about the state's libraries, as well as information on how to use the library and library careers. See the order form on the next page for title listings.

Special Library Resource Form

Subject	Library Town	Page # Reference
_____	_____	___,___,___,___,___
_____	_____	___,___,___,___,___
_____	_____	___,___,___,___,___
_____	_____	___,___,___,___,___
_____	_____	___,___,___,___,___
_____	_____	___,___,___,___,___
_____	_____	___,___,___,___,___
_____	_____	___,___,___,___,___
_____	_____	___,___,___,___,___
_____	_____	___,___,___,___,___
_____	_____	___,___,___,___,___

Special Library Resource Form

Subject	Library Town	Page # Reference
_____	_____	___,___,___,___
_____	_____	___,___,___,___,___
_____	_____	___,___,___,___,___
_____	_____	___,___,___,___,___
_____	_____	___,___,___,___,___
_____	_____	___,___,___,___,___
_____	_____	___,___,___,___,___
_____	_____	___,___,___,___,___
_____	_____	___,___,___,___,___
_____	_____	___,___,___,___,___
_____	_____	___,___,___,___,___
_____	_____	___,___,___,___,___

Special Library Resource Form

Subject	Library Town	Page # Reference
_____	_____	___,___,___,___,___
_____	_____	___,___,___,___,___
_____	_____	___,___,___,___,___
_____	_____	___,___,___,___,___
_____	_____	___,___,___,___,___
_____	_____	___,___,___,___,___
_____	_____	___,___,___,___,___
_____	_____	___,___,___,___,___
_____	_____	___,___,___,___,___
_____	_____	___,___,___,___,___
_____	_____	___,___,___,___,___
_____	_____	___,___,___,___,___

Special Library Resource Form

Subject	Library Town	Page # Reference
_____	_____	___,___,___,___,___
_____	_____	___,___,___,___,___
_____	_____	___,___,___,___,___
_____	_____	___,___,___,___,___
_____	_____	___,___,___,___,___
_____	_____	___,___,___,___,___
_____	_____	___,___,___,___,___
_____	_____	___,___,___,___,___
_____	_____	___,___,___,___,___
_____	_____	___,___,___,___,___
_____	_____	___,___,___,___,___
_____	_____	___,___,___,___,___

Special Library Resource Form

Subject	Library Town	Page # Reference
_____	_____	___,___,___,___,___
_____	_____	___,___,___,___,___
_____	_____	___,___,___,___,___
_____	_____	___,___,___,___,___
_____	_____	___,___,___,___,___
_____	_____	___,___,___,___,___
_____	_____	___,___,___,___,___
_____	_____	___,___,___,___,___
_____	_____	___,___,___,___,___
_____	_____	___,___,___,___,___
_____	_____	___,___,___,___,___
_____	_____	___,___,___,___,___

Special Library Resource Form

Subject	Library Town	Page # Reference
_____	_____	___,___,___,___,___
_____	_____	___,___,___,___,___
_____	_____	___,___,___,___,___
_____	_____	___,___,___,___,___
_____	_____	___,___,___,___,___
_____	_____	___,___,___,___,___
_____	_____	___,___,___,___,___
_____	_____	___,___,___,___,___
_____	_____	___,___,___,___,___
_____	_____	___,___,___,___,___
_____	_____	___,___,___,___,___
_____	_____	___,___,___,___,___

Special Library Resource Form

Subject	Library Town	Page # Reference
_____	_____	___,___,___,___,___
_____	_____	___,___,___,___,___
_____	_____	___,___,___,___,___
_____	_____	___,___,___,___,___
_____	_____	___,___,___,___,___
_____	_____	___,___,___,___,___
_____	_____	___,___,___,___,___
_____	_____	___,___,___,___,___
_____	_____	___,___,___,___,___
_____	_____	___,___,___,___,___
_____	_____	___,___,___,___,___
_____	_____	___,___,___,___,___

Special Library Resource Form

Subject	Library Town	Page # Reference
_____	_____	___,___,___,___,___
_____	_____	___,___,___,___,___
_____	_____	___,___,___,___,___
_____	_____	___,___,___,___,___
_____	_____	___,___,___,___,___
_____	_____	___,___,___,___,___
_____	_____	___,___,___,___,___
_____	_____	___,___,___,___,___
_____	_____	___,___,___,___,___
_____	_____	___,___,___,___,___
_____	_____	___,___,___,___,___
_____	_____	___,___,___,___,___

Special Library Resource Form

Subject	Library Town	Page # Reference
_____	_____	___,___,___,___,___
_____	_____	___,___,___,___,___
_____	_____	___,___,___,___,___
_____	_____	___,___,___,___,___
_____	_____	___,___,___,___,___
_____	_____	___,___,___,___,___
_____	_____	___,___,___,___,___
_____	_____	___,___,___,___,___
_____	_____	___,___,___,___,___
_____	_____	___,___,___,___,___
_____	_____	___,___,___,___,___
_____	_____	___,___,___,___,___

Special Library Resource Form

Subject	Library Town	Page # Reference
_____	_____	___,___,___,___,___
_____	_____	___,___,___,___,___
_____	_____	___,___,___,___,___
_____	_____	___,___,___,___,___
_____	_____	___,___,___,___,___
_____	_____	___,___,___,___,___
_____	_____	___,___,___,___,___
_____	_____	___,___,___,___,___
_____	_____	___,___,___,___,___
_____	_____	___,___,___,___,___
_____	_____	___,___,___,___,___
_____	_____	___,___,___,___,___,0